Funko Collecting:

According to a

Ghostwriter

Dedication

This book is dedicated to our fans.

Forward

Hi! This is Mike and I'm super excited to be writing this dope forward for a book we had written. We had this book written by someone else because neither Josh nor I are good at writing anything. So, here we are.

We paid some random user on Fiverr an undisclosed amount of money (More than $5 but less than $1000) to ghostwrite this whip. In Fact at the time of me writing this forward I haven't even read it. Irresponsible right? I heard people calling us mavericks... but I'm not sure if that's the case.

I'm not sure how to end these so… Forward Complete.

Preface

Are you looking to master the art of buying and selling collectible Funko Pops, or are you simply looking to learn more about their history, culture, or buying strategies?

Beginning your journey in the world of Funko Pops may be intimidating, as there are so many different avenues of collecting and trading them. By the end of this eBook, you will know the history of Pops, how to start buying them (if you haven't already), and a few exciting things you can do with your collection.

The Backstory

Before we begin, it is crucial to understand what Funko Pops are!

I'm sure you (*maybe unknowingly*) have an idea of what they are. Funko Pops are the cute figures that resemble characters from popular movies, sports teams, comics, and numerous other categories of pop culture. They are so much more than just cute displays though, they represent a *culture*, and an *art*.

Toy collector, Mike Becker came up with the idea based on his frustrations of looking for a product and not finding it. The first Funko product was a Big Boy coin bank. Unfortunately, this didn't take off, however, the idea to create bobbleheads quickly came and as did its success. After gaining a license to produce *Austin Powers* figures, the business started growing. The licensed products proved popular and the company added titles such as The Grinch.

In 2005, the company was sold and the new owner Brian Mariotti focused on growing the company's range of licensed merchandise and the first Funko POP was born. The first POP took the form of a classic Batman figure and was released at San Diego Comic-Con in 2010. Their big black lifeless eyes and oversized heads proved divisive, with some deeming them creepy while others found them endearing.

Taste aside the figures has become both an important and valued item among an enthusiastic collector's community. Funko POPs are available in many different shapes and sizes: most commonly 4", 6" or 10" to be exact, and come in a range of different finishes such as glossy and metallic. Some are even made to look invisible! Many collectors begin with buying their favorite characters. And then another, and another…. Before they know it, they are a Funko POP collector.

How to Begin

With over 8,000 Funko Pops being sold, it may feel a little overwhelming at first. Don't worry though, we'll walk you step by step through the process.

New collectors are advised against buying every character they see. Instead, they should stick to a theme of characters and try and finish them before moving on. This is particularly hard with ranges with lots of characters such as Star Wars or Disney. New collectors should start small, by focusing on a certain film perhaps.

*Understanding the "**Why**"!*

Whether it's to sell the collectible figurines or to create a stunning display of pops (which we'll discuss both later on), it is important to know why you want to collect. Make sure you have a clear idea of your goal.

The best way to start collecting Funko Pops is to begin with your personal favorites. With a cheap price tag on the figurines, it is easy to start your collection without stressing about the financial aspect. Build up your collection with your favorite characters and pops on the market. Most collectors begin with their favorite characters, and before they know it, their collection has already grown to 15 Funko Pops!

One of the best ways to go about purchasing your first Funko Pops is to shop at stores, such as Target, Walmart, and Barnes & Noble. Another effective way of finding Pops, which may lead you to find more unique and older Pops, is by shopping online.

Collectors and sellers are constantly selling online, and a good way to find the online stores is through Facebook groups, Reddit threads, and marketplace apps. If you choose to shop online though, make sure to be cautious of people who may be selling fake Funko Pops.

Identifying fake POPs

Unfortunately, the value of some POPs can attract the production of fakes. So, buyers and sellers must be vigilant and ensure that the product they are dealing with is legitimate. Luckily, there are a few easy guidelines to follow to help identify the authentic POPs from fakes.

1. **Retail box imperfections**: Disingenuous POPs tend to have tell-tale printing issues. Fakes tend to have a lower number placement on the right-hand-side of the box or line issues with the graphics on the box tend to appear. They may also have missing logos or stickers.

2. **Coloring on the POP**: Fake POPs look especially cheap compared to their licensed counterparts and coloring tends to be less vibrant.

3. **Foot stamp**: The number on the Funko POP retail boxes indicate the mould used in the

manufacturing process. Generally, legitimate POPs will have a stamp on the bottom of the foot that matches the box.

However, some of the most convincing fakes have successfully copied this, so this alone is not enough for definitive proof either way. It is a misconception that every legitimate POP has a matching stamp on both the foot and box. Funko has released official POPs without stamps, in cases where replacements were made because boxes were damaged during transit.

The Planet Arlia Vegeta from DragonballZ was quickly produced by Funko without foot stamps after a number were damaged on transit on the way to the New York Comic-Con in 2014 for the retailer to quickly swap.

Genuine Funko POPs should also have a Funko LLC logo on the foot. If it is not there, it may also below the rear skull or chin.

Although fake Pops is something to be aware of, buying online still has a lot of perks! When shopping online for Funkos, it is possible to find people selling internationally, which may lead to a broader selection to choose from. This can lead to finding unique and vintage characters. Remember, don't let the selection feel overwhelming! Choose the characters you like the best and continue your collecting journey from there.

Types of POPs

If you are looking to buy or sell, here are a few types of Funko POPs to look out for:

Exclusives

Despite the fact the majority of POPs are easily attainable, some Funko POPs are exclusive to specific stores or comic con conventions. There are many events that feature exclusive POP vinyls such as San Diego Comic and New York Comic Con.

They typically feature what is known as a *summer exclusive sticker* and is a little different from the convention sticker.

Products that are marked with an exclusive sticker can be sold for four-figure sums. However, it is important to note that licensing can differ from country to country. An American exclusive is not necessarily exclusive overseas. Some may be sent out to retailers to give international sellers a chance.

This category also includes figures exclusive to conventions and limited-number pieces. Pre- 2015 convention exclusives are amongst the highest valued. A series of three released for the 2010 San Diego Comic-Con including Batman, Batgirl, and Green Lantern. Only 480 Batman, 240 Batgirl, and 240 Green Lantern POPs were made. The most expensive is currently Green Lantern with some selling between £1000 and £1500 each.

Chases

Funko POPs with a "CHASE" sticker indicate that the figure is a rarer variant of a different POP. These types of figures are produced at a 1:6 ratio, meaning that there are five times as many common variants. Older pre-2015 chasers are considerably rarer as they were produced at a ratio of 1:36.

Originally, chasers would be the same figurine in a metallic or glow finish but these days Funko has begun to produce chasers which are a completely different design.

Vaulted

A "vaulted" POP is one that has been officially 'retired' by the company meaning that they will never be produced by Funko again. This type of POP will often shoot up value soon after it has been 'vaulted'. This status can be, at times, tricky to identify, and while the Funko app is a good place to start with, such a large online community asking around is a great place to start.

Protos

Proto POPS are usually unfinished versions from the production process. These are generally given away at official Funko events. The collection of these items has an entire sub-market dedicated to collecting them and are generally sold through private communities instead of eBay.

<u>Selling</u>

The world of selling Funko Pops can be competitive, and you must <u>stand out</u> to make it to the top of the market.

To make sure you have a Pop that will sell for your ideal prices, take a look around the current market! Prices will fluctuate, as new Pops are coming out and older ones are growing in value. If you have a figurine that is older, there is a good chance it has risen in value and may be worth looking into selling.

There are also different lines of Pops that will create more revenue than others. One type of Funko Pop that will have more value is Exclusive Pops.

When selling Pops, you need to know your audience.

There is a large international community of sellers, so if you're looking to increase the price on an exclusive figurine, make sure it is exclusive in the country of the buyer as well.

Timing is key!

Those looking to sell Funko POPs must time their sales well, as the market is almost completely based on 'buzz'. Ultimately value is based on *fan enthusiasm* for a new character or product release. Timing is everything! Keen sellers will have to act quickly as POPs are most valuable after release and will decrease in value dramatically within the first couple of months. Rather morbidly, whenever a celebrity dies, POPS of the characters they played often rise in value. Figures related to entertainment franchises will fluctuate with the popularity of the series.

For example, the best time to sell a Disney themed Pop would be when Disney makes an announcement. The excitement from the announcement will prompt Disney fans to buy more Disney-related merchandise, including Disney themed Pops. If you were selling a Disney Pop, you would then be able to raise the price of it when there is excitement around Disney. Selling is all about timing, so make sure to keep an eye out for announcements from Funko or from brands that your Pop is based on.

Sellers should also beware that the market generally experiences an annual dip around July and October around the time of San Diego Comic-Con and New York Comic-Con. Around this time collectors tend to sell off old POPs, to make way for new POPs they plan to buy at conventions. More casual sellers should definitely steer clear of these months.

Ultimately, Funko POPs are more valuable in their retail boxes, so potential sellers should handle their POPs with care as damage to them will decrease their sales values. This isn't to discourage collectors who want to display their Funko POPs around their home, just remember to keep the boxes and handle them with care.

Lastly, let's look at where to sell your Funko Pops.

<u>eBay</u>

eBay is the simplest platform for selling POPs. Sellers can list their POPs individually or in small lots to maximize their profits. For those looking to sell, eBay is also a great tool for deciding prices. The website's listings (including a dedicated category) are a great indicator of the market value of individual POPs through recent-sold listings. New buyers should definitely avoid supermarkets and other larger stores as they only sell less profitable mainstream POPs.

Poppriceguide.com is another great resource for aggerating prices from eBay and tracking the inventory of your collection.

Sellers using eBay should make sure to take a range of pictures to feature in the product listing including pictures of each side of the box. Honesty is the best policy in terms of any box damage and this should be detailed listing especially as POP collectors are famously picky about box damage. eBay also allows buyers to leave the product listing without much moderation, and can pretty be left alone apart from possible buyer questions.

However, eBay takes a 10% cut from the final value so it isn't for everyone. Alternatively, sellers may want to use the online marketplace Mercari which has over 999+ Funko listings.

Community Sale

Sellers can also make a **community sale** on dedicated online such as "Funko Trading" on Facebook or through the r/funkoswap subreddit thread. These spaces provide a platform for buyers, sellers, and traders to organize sales. An advantage of community selling is the heightened transparency. Due to the fact both buyers and sellers are accountable to the larger community, it is much more likely you are not dealing with scammers.

Community buying groups are perfect for finding interested buyers because chances are if someone has a special interest and is knowledgeable about POPs, they will be a group member. However, the major disadvantage of community selling is the engagement and effort required. Fundamentally, active groups require active sellers who are prepared for competition, accommodating requests, and responding to messages from interested buyers.

Lot Sales

Another way to sell POPs is through **lot sales**. Sellers can save both time and energy if they sell a collection of POPs in the one go. Large numbers can be sold at a discount to get rid of common pieces quickly. If you are looking to sell this way, smaller lots separated by a franchise can be sold on eBay but 7BucksAPop is recognized as the best place to sell collections. Some of these buyers can also be found in the POP community selling groups.

Although many buyers will be looking to make a profit, sellers should not disregard this method as it can prove helpful if you have a lot of common

POPs which would not sell quickly otherwise.

Buyers will often help out with shipping costs.

<u>Trading</u>

Trading is similar to both selling and buying, as you are receiving a new Pop in exchange for one of your Pops. When trading, it is essential to keep an eye out for fake Pops or for people who may be scamming you. As discussed earlier, people who are looking to profit may be going about it and using fake figurines. Make sure to look out for the same tell-tale signs that were mentioned in the buying section of this eBook.

When looking to trade, it is important to be very clear about what you have and what you want. This will also help you to avoid any miscommunications between you and the person you are trading with. If you aren't clear on what you have, it may upset the other person; if you don't clarify what you want to receive, you may end up getting something that is of no value. With trading, everyone will have a different idea about what they should trade their Pops for and what they're worth. The market is huge! If you don't agree with someone's trade-off, don't be afraid to look elsewhere. There will always be a market for what you are selling and what you are looking for.

<u>In Conclusion</u>

The art of buying, selling, and trading Funko Pops may seem like a lot, but we are here to guide you through the process, and so is the rest of the community. To sum up, here are a few key points:

- Don't feel pressured to buy certain Pops to begin. Start your collection with what you like!

- Displaying your Pops is a creative process. Make sure to tailor the display to the size of the collection and play around with it until you find what you think looks best.

- The two most important tips for selling your collection are to *know your audience* and *know when to sell it.*

- When trading, be as clear as possible about what you have and what you want.

Funko Pops is a global community that is constantly expanding in both members and collectible items. It is a personal journey, so enjoy it!

Best of luck to you and your future collection of Funko Pops.